May this book bless you beyond measure!
-CT-

Through my *Eyes*
from *His Spirit*

A FRESH PERSPECTIVE ON GOD'S WORD

CHARAE TUCKER

Print ISBN: 978-1-09831-368-5

eBook ISBN: 978-1-09831-369-2

ACKNOWLEDGEMENTS

To my parents Larry and Cherri Tucker—Thank you for believing in me. You both have always told me that whatever I want to do in life, I can. There are no limits. You have supported and loved me unconditionally since day one. I am blessed to have you both in my corner and there will never be enough words to express my gratitude for the years of love, support, prayers and sacrifices. I love you both so much!

To Samitriya—You pushed, encouraged and held me accountable throughout the entire writing process of this devotional. You understood the vision and importance of this from day one. Thank you for being my rock during one of my most challenging seasons of life and my place of solace when I needed it most. I am grateful for our friendship and excited to see what else unfolds for us!

To my family and friends—I love each of you dearly and appreciate the moments I have shared will all of you. The impact you each have had on my life does not go unnoticed. Thank you for every prayer, words of encouragement and laughs we have shared.

FOREWORD

As a father, my worst nightmare occurred when my son was a toddler. He was eating at the table and he began to cough. I quickly noticed that he was turning red and could not catch his breath. I quickly removed the food that was blocking his airway. Once we all calmed down, I demonstrated the importance of bite size pieces. The scriptures say that this life is short and full of trouble. Our own selfish desires, lack of self-control and free-will coupled with sin, grief and disappointment can cause us as Christians to feel as though we are suffocating at times. We need to be reminded to take bite size pieces of God's word every day. This devotional should be approached as a spiritual meal that is easily digested for growth and proper nutrition.

So, whether your devotional life is flourishing, struggling or nonexistent this devotional is for you. It is my prayer that you embrace this devotional as a feast that you will enjoy in bite size pieces. If you experience each day afresh, digest the themes, and meditate on the word of God, then the scriptures say that the LORD will give you the desires of your heart.

Ms. Charae Tucker, is on assignment like all of us who follow Christ. She has been mandated to share the gospel and her testimony. Charae carries out this mandate on the pages of this devotional. The scriptures instruct us to meditate on the law both day and night. Ms. Charae Tucker, in her thirty-day devotional assists readers with daily meditation. Thought provoking personal reflections and life altering convictions make this devotional unique and relatable.

Enjoy the journey!

S. Michael Greene

Student, Preacher, Bible Teacher

NOTE FROM THE AUTHOR

I am excited that you have this devotional in your hands! My goal when writing it was simply to be obedient to God. Every word on these pages are truly from His Spirit. He longs to connect with you in a deeper way and because nothing happens by chance, you are meant to have this devotional in your hands.

I hope that before you start, you set your intention to be transparent, vulnerable and open to receiving the special word that God has specifically for you. The questions at the end of each day are the same questions that God has asked me. They will challenge you to look deep within, get real with yourself and God and ultimately push you closer towards the purpose He has for you.

I encourage you to share this with a friend or group of friends who are also looking for more depth in their relationship with God. Now let's get started!

Sincerely,

Charae Tucker

DAY 1

Who Sent You?

"Have I not commanded you? Be strong and courageous! Do not tremble or be dismayed, for the Lord, your God, is with you wherever you go."
–Joshua 1:9

Background: After Moses' death, God calls Joshua to take over in leading the Israelites to the Promised Land. He's promoted from 'assistant' to the leader of over 2 million people. Not only does God call Joshua but He reaffirms that He will be with him, as He was with Moses and He will give him victory over his enemies and favor every step of the way (v.1-5).

I imagine that when it came time for Joshua to step into this new assignment, he was nervous, fearful, and perhaps somewhat doubtful of his capabilities. And if he wasn't, I'm sure Satan was planting seeds of doubt in his mind. But God comes to him and says, "Have I not commanded you?" To fully trust God at his word and walk into our assignment with authority, we must remember and understand who God really is. We have to remember his track record in our lives. When God gives us an assignment, we should not be hindered by the difficulty of it but instead be encouraged by who is sending us. He is not going to send us into an assignment without proper preparation. Keep in mind, preparation may not always look how you think it should, nor does it only include you. God will also prepare the place where you will be going and the people you will encounter.

I worked for Peloton Cycle, an in-home tech fitness brand. They offer spin classes at an NY studio, which users can stream into. When God told me to apply there, I was confused. I didn't even know what spin classes were. But I obeyed and when I got the position, God not only equipped me with the ability to learn what I needed to be successful but He also prepared the way for me. I was shown so much favor while working for the company. And God used my time there to propel me into the next major season of my life: full time entrepreneurship.

No matter what your assignment might be, remember who has commanded you and draw your strength and courage from that. Just as God promised to be with Joshua wherever he went, be assured the same promise applies to you.

What assignment has God given you that you need to exercise more faith and less fear in?

Focus & Reflect

....

....

....

....

....

....

....

....

....

....

....

....

....

....

....

....

....

DAY 2

Set Apart

"And do not be conformed to this world, but be transformed by the renewing of your mind, so that you may prove what the will of God is, that which is good and acceptable and perfect." –Romans 12:2

Background: Paul is writing to the church in Rome, which he has not yet visited. He starts by explaining the foundation and essence of the Christian faith. In the remaining chapters, he gives practical guidelines on how the church should live in a sinful world.

Just as Christians then were called to be set apart (John 15:19, II Corinthians 5:17, I Peter 2:9, I John 4:5-6), we too are called to be set apart and not be 'conformed to this world.' As I started to grow in my walk with Christ, one of my greatest challenges was accepting the responsibility that comes with being set apart. "God, how do I change these behaviors that are not a reflection of You; especially the ones I have no desire to change?" God taught me that change starts from within and flows outward. As our minds are renewed through Christ, our actions and behaviors begin to naturally change to reflect Him as opposed to the world.

Renewing my mind meant taking a look at what I was feeding it. I'm sure you're familiar with the saying 'you are what you eat' or 'what you put in is what you get out.' The same is true in our walk with Christ. I had to increase my spiritual food and decrease my worldly food. As I did that, not only did my appetite change but my behavior started to change, too. A lot of habits that I was struggling to change or rid myself of started gradually changing on their own. Often, we make the mistake of putting pressure on ourselves to change but that's not on us. It's God who does the transforming; we are to love Him and surrender to Him. It's in full surrender that He is able to transform us. The more time we spend with God, the more we naturally begin to surrender.

Knowing Him better also comes by spending time with Him. Think about your longest, closet friend. You've known them for so long, I'm sure you're able to tell when they are in a certain mood or have something on their mind. You can discern when something is off. That's what Paul is saying in this verse: through our transformation and spending more time with God, we are able to discern what His will is for our lives.

What behaviors do you need to change to be more like Christ? Write them down, give them to God and then, shift your focus from those habits to spending more time with Him. Release your grip on that behaviour so that God can complete His work in you.

Focus & Reflect

....

....

....

....

....

....

....

....

....

....

....

....

....

....

....

....

DAY 3

Comfort in Waiting

*"Rest in the Lord and wait patiently for Him;
do not fret because of him who prospers in his
way, because of the man who carries out wicked
schemes." –Psalm 37:7*

Background: The book of Psalms is comprised of songs, written mainly by David. In Chapter 37, written by David, he addresses the prosperity of the wicked compared to the sometimes hardships or lack of success of the righteous.

What does it mean to 'rest?' It means to 'be still.' Be still in the Lord (Psalm 46:10). When I think of resting, I think of Sundays on the couch with my favorite blanket, watching a movie, without a care in the world. In the same way, as we 'rest' in the Lord, we should be unbothered by current trials or how things seem to be or not to be working out. We should be comfortable in our waiting, secure, and ready to move, only when God says to. Can I be real though? I'm not good at waiting and have identified a pattern of it.

When God tells me to wait, my first reaction is usually apprehension, followed with a list of questions. Then, after trying things my way, and usually making a mess, I transition into a period of settling into waiting and resting in Him and His timing. But if too much time starts to pass by, I start to get anxious. I shift my focus from Him, back to my circumstances and then, I isolate Him. When I'm isolated from Him, even though He may still speak to me, the reception is bad and I start making decisions based on emotions and not His word.

But how are we supposed to wait? We are to wait patiently. Another translation reads, '…wait longingly' so we should wait longingly in anticipation but not be anxious. What does that look like? I think it's a mindset. Longing to hear from God so bad that moving prior to hearing from Him isn't an option. It means being so excited for His word that you don't have time to entertain the negative thoughts of others or yourself. Being so excited about what He has in store for you that you dare not take measures into your own hands.

Lastly, we are not to be concerned with how God is moving in the lives of others around us. God has a specific plan for each of us, tailored to our unique being.

What is your waiting pattern? Once you identify it, you can start breaking the unhealthy cycle and start waiting patiently and longingly on the One who holds all the answers.

Focus & Reflect

....

....

....

....

....

....

....

....

....

....

....

....

....

....

....

....

DAY 4

Bold Despite Fear

"For God has not given us a spirit of timidity, but of power and love and discipline." –II Timothy 1:7

Background: II Timothy is a letter Paul writes to encourage Timothy. God has given Timothy a gift (God has given all of us gifts to be used for ministry) and Paul encourages him to use His gift boldly.

God has given all of us gifts and unique callings to exercise those gifts within. While the bible does not specify what Timothy's gift was, we know he was called to lead the church at Ephesus. I remember when God called me to be one of the young adult leaders for a mid-week grow group at my church. Whew, scary! I never had a desire to lead anything at church and was just beginning to become comfortable with going and participating in discussions. But I've learned that when God calls, it's best to answer the first time. This is one of the scriptures I leaned on during my new assignment. I have also continued to lean on it whenever I face a new task or am entering into a new season that is outside of my comfort zone. So, how does this 'power,' 'love,' and 'discipline' practically translate into our lives?

Power: Courage to do what frightens us; a firm decision to do what we've been called to do and not be held back by anything or anyone. Sometimes being bold doesn't mean eliminating fear but it means doing what you're called to do, despite the fear.

Love: Our love for God should set us above the fear of failure. Our love for Him should be so much so that we answer the call He has placed on our lives no matter what. Love drives action. Act on what God has called you to do.

Sound mind: This means a quietness of mind. Not allowing our imagination and fear of failure to discourage us in doing what God has placed on our hearts to do. We have to get out of our own heads and quiet the noise that seeks to steal our peace of mind.

Out of power, love and a sound mind, which do you have the most difficulty tapping into and why? Write down a current situation and two practical ways you can apply the quality you are struggling with the most.

DAY 5

Our Power Source

"Remain in Me and I will remain in you. For a branch cannot produce fruit if it is severed from the vine, and you cannot be fruitful unless you remain in Me. Yes, I am the vine; you are the branches. Those who remain in Me, and I in them, will produce much fruit. For apart from Me, you can do nothing." –John 15:4-5

Background: Jesus is speaking to His disciples, preparing them for His death and resurrection. He uses parables to teach them how to live and carry on the ministry once He is gone.

When we plug our charger into our phone, we also plug the other end into the switch. If we don't, the phone won't charge. We don't expect our TV to turn on if it's not plugged into the wall socket, the source of its power. In fact, we don't expect any of our electronic items to work if they are not connected to the power source. Yet, for some reason, we expect to be fruitful and accomplish our goals without being connected to our power source, the true vine, Jesus.

No matter how talented, equipped or prepared we are to carry out a task or accomplish a goal, if we are not connected to Jesus, our source, we will not bear any fruit. If we do bear fruit, it will only be a fraction of what we could've produced. Owning a business has been challenging and at times frustrating. A lot of the frustration comes when I'm not seeing the desired results from the time and effort I've been investing. What I've noticed though, is in those times, I have not been connected to the vine. I've been operating on my own strength. Somewhere down the line, I started operating without God. When this happens, it seems as if I'm just spinning my wheels, trying to 'make it happen.'

The truth is, where God has called us, there is no room for failure. The real 'secret of success,' is staying connected to the true vine, the real source of our power flow.

Our connection to Him must be ongoing, not only while we are praying to receive. It's unwise to pray diligently for something and once we receive it, to not remain in prayer and connected. Then, we can't properly manage what we have received.

What areas of your life are you not bearing fruit in or are yielding less than expected? Are you still connected to the vine? If not, how can you reconnect to the power source, God?

Focus & Reflect

DAY 6

Too Busy to Pray

"...and he kneeled upon his knees 3 times a day
and prayed and gave thanks before God."
–Daniel 6:10

Background: Daniel and the Jews are living in captivity in Babylon. However, God has given Daniel favor amongst the King. In this verse specifically, Daniel is praying, even after a decree has been signed that for 30 days no one should pray to anyone except the King. If this decree were violated then the person or persons would be thrown into the lion's den. Despite this, Daniel still continues to pray three times a day.

As much as God has going on, running the entire world and keeping track of the hairs on our heads, we don't ever expect Him to be too busy to answer our prayers. But somehow, we constantly find ourselves too busy to talk to Him. We fail to realize how important consistent and transparent communication is in our relationship with God, just as it is in our earthly relationships. We all have at least one person we will sacrifice time for to speak with, no matter what we have going on. I bet the person that just came to mind wasn't God. No judgment, it's not the first person that came to my mind either.

Despite being in a spiritual warfare (Ephesians 6:11-17; II Corinthians 10:3-5) and facing daily challenges, we find ourselves too busy to commune with God. How can we expect to win a war if we're not communicating with the Sergeant? How can we be successful in the game of life if we don't communicate with the playmaker? We are quick to get annoyed or upset when someone doesn't return a call or text. Or worse, when we see someone active on social media but they haven't texted us back. How do you think God feels seeing us going about our daily lives, talking to our friends and commenting on posts of strangers we will likely never meet? He is longing to hear from us and talk to us. Will we make time for Him?

Daniel faced being thrown in the lion's den if he was caught praying and yet, still he prayed, three times a day! If you continue to read this chapter, you'll find that Daniel was eventually thrown into the lion's den. However, he was unharmed. A lot of times, we fail to pause and spend time with God because we feel we have more pressing issues to dedicate our time to. Maybe, we don't want to miss out on something, get behind, or further behind, on our schedules, etc. But we must come to realize and truly believe that when we start with God first and keep Him at the center of our lives, He takes care of everything else. Life just flows smoother. (Psalm 84:11) And in our times of prayer, we gain insight, direction and clarity on how to handle our day or certain issues we are facing.

What keeps you from communicating with God more? Yes, I know you're busy but dig deeper. What are your subconscious thoughts or feelings about communicating with God that keep you from making time for Him?

Focus & Reflect

DAY 7

Meditation

"But his delight is in the law of the Lord and in His law he mediates day and night." –Psalms 1:2

Background: The first chapter of the Psalms, specifically illustrates life's two roads, the life of the godly with the ungodly and those in a relationship with God, as opposed to those not in a relationship with Him. We see in this verse that a child of God delights and meditates on God's word.

In a relationship, we often think about the other person, reread text messages that make us blush and send a tingling feeling through our body. We enjoy spending time with them and thinking of ways to spend more time with them. If we are having a stressful day, we may even think about that person as a way to escape. This is the same attitude we should have about God and His word. It should pleasure us to hear from Him and mediate on His words. He wants to be our escape when life is tearing us apart. He wants us to delight in and find joy spending time with Him. We can become so focused and sometimes obsessed with finding happiness in someone else when God is the only who can truly fill that void or desire.

There are numerous benefits to mediating on God's word. One, we start to understand His character and know the sound of His voice. So many times, I've been guilty of complaining that God isn't talking to me or about not being able to clearly hear or understand what He's saying. In our world today, there are so many distractions that it can become confusing as to whom we are hearing from and what is influencing our decisions. Is it God, social media, friends, family or a combination of everyone? We need to turn down the volume of the world and turn up the volume on God and His word.

What do you find yourself meditating on the most? What thoughts are constantly running through your mind? Begin focusing on being more aware of your thoughts throughout the various segments of your day. When you notice your mind entertaining thoughts that are not edifying, switch your focus back to God, what He's been speaking to you and the truths of His word.

Focus & Reflect

....

....

....

....

....

....

....

....

....

....

....

....

....

....

....

....

DAY 8

Your Season is Coming

"And he shall be like a tree planted by the rivers of water, that bringeth forth his fruit in his season; his leaf also shall not wither; and whatsoever he doeth shall prosper." –Psalms 1:3

Background: Today, we pick up from yesterday's key verse, where we learned one characteristic of a child of God, is that he or she meditates on His word. In this verse we learn the effect of meditating on His word.

The person that meditates on the work of God is not only blessed, but he will yield fruit in his season. The person who plants themselves at the feet of Jesus, surrendered to His will, they will yield fruit, in their season. Those 3 words are very important. Just as a tree bears fruit in a specific season, you and I bear fruit *in our season*. That's why it is imperative to mediate on the word of God and not the social media page of other people and the fruit they appear to be yielding.

Looking at what other people are producing, or the perception of what other people are producing, can cause us to grow impatient with God. I'm not sure about you but when I begin to get impatient with God, I stop surrendering to Him and start doing things my way. My way and timing always results in a longer process and unnecessary loss.

While writing this, I'm on Day 9 of a 40-day social media fast. I'm taking time away from social media for several reasons. One of them is because I started looking at the success of others in a way that was frustrating me and not motivating me. I started questioning God on when my breakthrough was coming. This verse reminds me that it's not a question of if I will bear fruit but when. And the 'when' is during 'my season.' You too will bear your fruit, in your season. So meditate on God's word and not on the success of others. It's during meditation that you will find God's peace to calm you, His provision to keep you and His power to persevere. You will also get direction from Him on what you need to work on to be prepared to bear and sustain the fruit you are so desperately praying for.

What vision has God given you? Write it down, along with the qualities, mindset and lifestyle changes needed to manifest the vision and manage it when it comes to pass.

Focus & Reflect

....

....

....

....

....

....

....

....

....

....

....

....

....

....

....

Let God Show Out

"The Lord said to Gideon, 'The people who are
with you are too many for Me to give Midian into
their hands, for Israel would be boastful saying,
'my own power has delivered me.''" – Judges 7:2

Background: The book of Judges spans over 325 years and details the account of the Israelites in the Promised Land. However, because of sin and disobedience, they continually found themselves captive to other nations. In Chapter 7, they are currently under the rule of the Midianites. Gideon has gathered over 30,000 men to fight and overtake Midian. However, God says that is too many men. God knew that if they won the battle with that many men, they would take the credit for themselves and He would not receive the glory. Over the next few verses, Gideon narrows down his army from 30,000 men to 300 men! It is then that God delivers victory to them over the Midianites.

This passage is a great reminder to me that it's all about God getting the glory! As I look over my own life, I'm reminded of the same. While rebuilding my finances, I often find myself thinking, how easy it would be if God blessed me with a large sum of money. I could pay off all my debts at once, travel, give back, invest, grow my business, and the list goes on. But that's not the plan God has nor would that plan give Him the most glory. It would easily become about the money and not about the ways in which God provided and sustained me during this time. A large sum of money would stop me from experiencing God in ways like never before. It would stop me from seeing His creativity and power. It would rob Him of the opportunity to 'boss up' in my life in a major way.

Many people doubted Gideon's decision to dwindle his army down from 30,000 men to 300. Gideon most likely had his own apprehensions but he was obedient and kept moving forward; and we see what God did, he gave them the victory. When God gives us a vision, we have to trust him to help us make it a reality, in His way and in His timing. It may not look like we have what we need or God may ask us to give up or walk away from the very thing or person we think we need. But the truth is, all we need is Him and all He needs is our trust.

What are you waiting on God to deliver you from or do in your life? Ask that God would open your heart to fully receive His plan and timing for what you're expecting. Ask that He give you the courage to give up what you think you need and place your full trust in Him.

Focus & Reflect

....

....

....

....

....

....

....

....

....

....

....

....

....

....

....

....

DAY 10

Let God In

*"Your eyes have seen my unformed substance;
and in your book were all written, the days that
were ordained for me when as yet there was not
one of them." –Psalm 139:16*

Background: In this chapter, the writer details God's all-seeing and all-knowing character. God know us better than we know ourselves and still invites us to know Him, despite our unworthiness.

Why do we try to hide from God? Why do we mask our feelings instead of being transparent with Him? He knew us when we were but a substance (Jeremiah 1:5). Imagine, being nothing but matter, fluid in the womb. Even in that state, He knew us, who we would become and He loved us still. That should give us confidence to bare it all before Him, without hesitation. I came across a tweet from Christian Rap Artist Lecrae that read, "…He wants to walk with you through the pain, not just make it disappear." I felt that on so many levels.

We can be so quick to ask God to deliver us from situations, provide us with things we lack and give us clarity and peace of mind. We are basically asking for a Band-Aid instead of healing. But we call family members or friends, or hop on social media and vent about the problem, hoping for insight from them. But guess who actually wants to hear about all of that? God. He is the only one who gives us the insight we need. (I'm not suggesting that God does have people in our lives that can give us godly wisdom and advice but God should be the first one we go to). He also understands us more than any of those people ever will. He's seen us when were nothing, an "unformed substance," so don't hide from Him now. He is developing you into who He has ordained you to be.

He already has the solution for what you are going through, now grab his hand and let Him lead you. And maybe you aren't consciously hiding from him. I'm guilty of keeping my emotions to myself. My emotions sometimes get buried so deep that I forget they exist. But God doesn't forget. He wants to talk with us about whatever that 'thing' is we've been sweeping under the rug.

Let me give you a good example of digging deeper. In the past, I've asked God to help me move on from a relationship. I had to dig deeper to realize I was having trouble moving on because of guilt that I was inadequate, which stemmed from situations from my childhood. That's digging deep but that's what God wants. Sure, He can and did help me move on from that relationship but He was also able to help me heal from a much bigger issue, an issue that would have negatively impacted future relationships.

What has life recently thrown your way that has you stressed or unsure about? Instead of calling your go-to person or getting on twitter, write it out to God or begin to talk to Him out loud about how you really feel, dig deep. He wants to hear from you.

Focus & Reflect

DAY 11

Leaving the Familiar

"Now the Lord said to Abram, 'Go forth from your country, and from your relatives and from your father's house, to the land which I will show you; and I will make you a great nation, and I will bless you, and make your name great; and so you shall be a blessing.'" –Genesis 12:1-2

Background: During this time, Abram is living in Ur with his family. This is also the first time Abram receives the promise of having descendants as many as the stars. However, to initiate the manifestation of the promise, he had to pack up his family and leave behind his relatives and home.

God promises Abram a great nation but he first he had to leave the comforts of home. His blessing was dependent on his obedience. He had to leave the familiar in order to receive greater from God and be used in a greater way. Blessings require obedience. What is your familiar? Where are you most comfortable? We must be willing to fully surrender to God's instruction, to receive His best for us. This sometimes means even without fully knowing what His plan is.

Obedience has to be unconditional. We need to be willing to obey regardless of knowing or understanding what God is up to. God promises Abram something amazing: a great nation would come from him; He would be blessed and his name would be great. But there's a catch: he had to leave his hometown and head to Canaan. Imagine, you have a great job, but God gives you a vision of something greater and the first thing He asks of you is to quit your job.

Well, not only did God tell Abram to leave home, He sent Him to Canaan. Canaan was small in dimension and wouldn't be the ideal place one would expect to start a great nation. However, God saw otherwise and Canaan ended up being the focal point for most of the history of Israel and had a tremendous impact on world history. And it was there that God established Abraham. Not only must we obey God but also humble ourselves as well. Isaiah 55:8-9 reads, 'for my thoughts are not your thoughts nor are your ways My ways,' declares the Lord. 'For as the heavens are higher than the earth, so are my ways higher than the earth, so are my ways higher than your ways and my thoughts than your thoughts.' He is always up to something greater than we could ever imagine.

Where is God telling you to go or what is He telling you to do? But because it seems insignificant to you, you won't go? You're asking for a breakthrough but are you willing to give up what you have now, to receive it?

Focus & Reflect

....
....
....
....
....
....
....
....
....
....
....
....
....
....
....
....
....

DAY 12

God Our Foundation

"Unless the Lord builds the house, they labor in vain who build it; unless the Lord guards the city, the watchman keeps awake in vain." –Psalm 127:1

Background: Solomon writes this Psalm as a reminder that life without God is senseless. Everything we do must have God at the foundation if we expect for our efforts to be worthwhile or successful.

If God's hand is not in what we are working on or if he has not ordered our steps, then we are wasting our time. In 2013, I decided I was going to move to Los Angeles in pursuit of becoming a Wardrobe Stylist. Not a bad idea, right? I studied fashion in college, worked in retail management and even invested time and money in attaining a wardrobe styling certification. I prayed about my decision but in hindsight, my prayer was not for direction or insight but for God to bless what I had already decided to do. So, off to LA I went. Things started off well but despite my efforts and small successes, less than a year later, I found myself moving back to Dallas. See, God was not the builder of that decision, I was. Despite the hard work I put in, trying to make a name for myself in LA, I did not achieve the success I planned on.

God knows what is best and the best timing for things to happen in our lives. He's been here longer and is more experienced (Colossians 1:15-17). When we attempt to do things on our own, we actually delay the process of what He is trying to do in our lives. Sometimes, we may even veer down the wrong path.

Waiting on God can sometimes feel like an impossible task, especially the further away our life seems to go from our timeline. However, when we begin to grow impatient with God, it's imperative that we remember His character. He is not withholding or delaying blessings out of spite or some senseless reason. He is preparing us, preparing the way and preparing the place we are going.

We can spend all the resources available to us to achieve our goals but in the end it will be a waste. We might succeed but what will it cost us in the end? Will we be able to sustain that success?

Think about what you are currently working on. It might be a special project, a promotion at work, a relationship or a new business idea. Have you surrendered it to God to see if it's in alignment with His will? Take time in prayer to surrender and dedicate what you're working on to God. Ask for His guidance and commit to aligning yourself to His will.

Focus & Reflect

DAY 13

Beauty in the Pain

*"My brethren, count it all joy when you fall into
various trials..." –James 1:2*

Background: James writes this book of the bible to Christians to remind
them their lives should reflect their relationship with Him. Genuine faith,
or relation with God will produce good deeds. At this time Christians were
also being persecuted because of their faith, and James is giving instruction
on how they should handle the various trials they face.

How many times have you heard this verse referenced in sermons? Most
times when I've heard it, it was at a time when I least wanted to hear it.
It's usually not until after I overcome the trial, that I have an "aha" and
understand why I had to go through what I did. Had I been mindful that
something greater was being produced in me, I would've had a positive
attitude about it.

When we want to get stronger, we lift weights. Let's say we start lifting a set
of 10lb dumbbells. Eventually, that is no longer difficult. So, we might move
up to a set of 15lb weights. Again, we experience pain and struggle like
before with the 10lb weights. But we're working on getting stronger, right?
Therefore, we've got to keep lifting heavier and heavier weights.

It's the same with the trials we go through in life. Think of the trial as a
workout. We've all asked God to be better and receive better in various
areas of our lives. One desire I expressed to God is to have unshakeable

faith in Him, and to follow His direction without hesitation. Well that is not accomplished without going through certain trials.

But remember, it's about getting stronger. God asked me, "Can I trust you to give your business back to me, while you focus on writing your first devotional?" (Yes, the one you have in your hands now). That was scary for me and I had a lot of questions! However, we must embrace our challenges and trials, they're simply a workout to strengthen us. I think it's a love/hate relationship. No, it doesn't feel good but knowing that you're getting better, getting closer to who you are working to be, that feels good. So, find the joy in your trials like James suggests here. If you continue reading this chapter, you'll see he goes into detail about the results of enduring trials. So be encouraged!

Think about what trial(s) you are currently in the midst of. How can it strengthen you and get you closer to being who you need to be in order to receive greater?

Focus & Reflect

DAY 14

The Refiner's Fire

*"For He is like a refiner's fire and like fullers' soap.
He will sit as a smelter and purifier of silver, and
He will purify the sons of Levi..." –Malachi 3:2-3*

Background: The book of Malachi is written to the people in Jerusalem. At the time, the majority of them are consumed in a life a sin. The people of Jerusalem are being rebuked, urged to repent and reminded that they serve a forgiving God.

You might be thinking, 'What in the world do the sons of Levi have to do with me?' That's not my focus here. My focus is on the characteristic of God that is mentioned. 'He is like a refiner's fire;' a refiner's fire is used to purify metal, by heating it until it melts. Once melted, all the scum rises to the top. Fullers' soap was caustic (able to burn or corrode organic tissue) and was used to produce bright white clothing.

Like the refiner's fire, God seeks to purify us and make us without blemish (as much as possible on this side of heaven). There is nothing that He cannot redeem us from, no matter what our past is, no matter what our present situation is. If you are reading this, you are not too far away from God's reach, to be refined or made new. I can't promise that it will be easy but I can promise His love, guidance, peace and restoration on the other side of the fire.

It starts with the realization of our wrongdoing(s) and then acknowledgement of our role in it. Next, comes confession, asking for forgiveness and help with changing our behavior and righting our wrongs. No matter what vice you might have, how long you've had it or how much you actually enjoy it, God can and wants to purify you and make you more like Him. He is waiting to refine us and burn away our fleshly and worldly desires.

What in your life do you feel like you can never be redeemed from? Have an honest conversation with God about it and ask the Holy Spirit to open you up and help you to surrender to the process of purification.

Focus & Reflect

DAY 15

Confidence

"For the Lord will be your confidence and will
keep your foot from being caught." –Proverbs 3:26

Background: Mostly written by Solomon, the purpose of Proverbs was to teach the people of Israel wisdom, how to attain it and apply it to everyday life. The book also covers other virtues such as discipline and prudent living.

One thing that was a constant struggle in my life was overcoming paralyzing fear. There were many times when I would let fear get the best of me, which would hinder the work God was trying to do through me. I would find myself doing so much "planning" that I was never actually doing anything. Subconsciously, I was avoiding stepping outside of my comfort zone. I was also only relying on myself, not God. I was focused on my limited knowledge and experience as opposed to the unlimited and unmatched power of God. I was not thinking about where my strength came from or whom I served.

It was confidence in myself that was hindering me. Self-confidence is important but it can't be the only source of our confidence. Nor should we have more confidence in ourselves than we do in God.

Once we take our confidence out of our human abilities and place it in God, we can be at peace. This verse tells us that He will keep our feet from being caught. For me, it means that He will keep me from partnerships that are not beneficial, relationships that are not edifying and business endeavors that our not in alignment with my greater purpose. He will do the same for you, as it pertains to the path you're on but you have to place your confidence in Him. Once you are able to do that, the fear begins to dissipate and the pessimistic voices in your head quiet down.

What do you place the most confidence in? Your job, salary, degree, connections, or looks? Imagine how life would change if you placed your confidence in God and relied more on Him?

Focus & Reflect

How Well Do You Really Know God?

"With all my heart I have sought You..."
–Psalm 119:10

Background: Psalm Chapter 119 is dedicated to glorifying God and His word. It refers back to other scriptures over and over again. It highlights the benefits of the word of God, meditating on it and the effects of being guided by it. In this particular verse, we see the priority the Psalmist placed on seeking God.

A couple of years ago, during a bible study series at my church, we studied from the book, 'The Names of God.' Each entry or chapter is a study on one of the 52 names of God. It explains the meaning of the name, references a key passage, followed by questions to help you explore and relate it to your life. As I studied some these names, the saying, 'There is Power in the name of Jesus,' takes on an entirely different meaning for me.

For us, different names/nicknames each mean something different or emphasizes a certain characteristic and evokes different emotions when we hear them. If I were in trouble growing up, my mom would call me by my full name. If I'm around family, I have a certain name I'm called (if you know, then you know). In high school, I was 'Shakey' (originated from being on the track team). Only about 2 people still call me that to this day but when I hear it, it takes me back to my HS days and gives me a nostalgic feeling. You probably have a nickname or two you're called, each representing something unique about you.

Well, it's the same with God. When I found out that He had 52 names, I was curious to know more. What were these names? What did they mean? How was I in a relationship with God and didn't know all His characteristics? The more I began to study, the closer I became to God and the more access I had to His power in my life.

The more we get to know a person, the greater potential of their impact on our life. The same is true with God, except there is not potential. He will have a tremendous impact on our lives. But we have to allow space for that, we have to commune with Him and spend time really getting to know Him, seek Him with all our heart.

About how much of uninterrupted time do you spend with God each week? If you are in a relationship or were in a relationship, would that be an acceptable amount of time for your partner to spend with you? Commit to increasing the time you spend with God, it can be as little as three minutes more a day. Don't get caught up in the number, it will naturally increase as your relationship evolves with Him.

....

....

....

....

....

....

....

....

....

....

....

....

....

....

....

DAY 17

Protect Your Energy

"Then the foreign rabble who were traveling with the Israelites began to crave the good things of Egypt. And the people of Israel also began to complain. 'Oh, for some meat!' they exclaimed. 'We remember the fish we used to eat for free in Egypt. And we had all the melons, leeks, onions and garlic we wanted. But now our appetites are gone. All we ever see is this manna!'" –Numbers 11:4-6

Background: After being delivered from Egypt as slaves, the Israelites head into the wilderness en route to the Promised Land. When the Israelites left Egypt, there were some Egyptians who left with them as well. They are the 'foreign rabble' referred to in this verse. The Israelites had already been punished a few verses prior and here they are again, complaining. But this time, it's the Egyptians who started the complaining and then the Israelites joined in.

Don't allow outside negative energy to change your perspective on how God is working in your life.

The Israelites had been held captive in Egypt for about 400 years. They cried out to God continuously to deliver them from the hand of Pharaoh (Exodus 2:23; 3:9) and because of their cry, God rescued them. In Egypt, they were living as slaves in the harshest conditions (Exodus 1:8-14). Now all of a sudden, the Egyptians who were traveling with them started complaining, and they began to complain too.

However, the Egyptians lived a different life in Egypt than the Israelites: they were not slaves. They were not subject to harsh living conditions, the lives of their male children were not threatened, and they were not beaten daily for not meeting impossible quotas.

Do not let the grumblings of other people make you grumble against God. It's easy to become ungrateful and forget what He has delivered us from. We can't afford to be influenced by negative energy. We must stay focused on God and what He has already done in our lives. Don't be tricked into thinking that where you were delivered from is better than where God is trying to take you.

Who or what have you been allowing to obstruct your view of the grace God has bestowed you and the amazing work that He is doing in your life? What blessings have you overlooked because they are not packaged they way you expected them to be?

Focus & Reflect

....

....

....

....

....

....

....

....

....

....

....

....

....

....

....

DAY 18

Faith Over Logic

"Trust in the Lord with all your heart and do not lean on your own understanding." –Proverbs 3:5

Background: Mostly written by Solomon, the purpose of Proverbs was to teach the people of Israel wisdom, how to attain it and apply it to everyday life. This chapter speaks on the rewards of wisdom.

At some point in my journey of being a full time entrepreneur, there was a time when I applied to about 10 jobs. I quickly moved to the first step of the interview process with two of the companies. After that, I heard nothing. Honestly, I was surprised that more companies had not contacted me.

I finally received two emails back from two of the companies, to schedule an interview. I wasted no time. In the middle of getting ready for the first interview, I was led in that moment to read over the job description again. As I was reading through it, there was an impression upon my spirit from God saying, 'You don't need to go to this interview, this is not what I have for you.' But I needed that job and I was not going to surrender that easily, I needed to be sure God was sure.

The conversation I had with God went something like this:

Me: But God…you know my current financial situation and how I've been eagerly looking for any opportunity to bring in some income.

God: But, I don't want just anything for you.

Me: There's no way this logically makes any sense!

God: But I am not a God of logic. I am of the Supernatural. I know what your needs are and I will continue to cover you, as I have been. You are where you are now for doing what you wanted and what you thought was best. And now you want to dictate to me how to deliver you?

I cancelled the interview.

As Lysa TerKeurst writes in her book, 'What Happens When Women Say Yes to God,' "[Surrendering] to God means making the choice to trust Him even when you can't understand why He requires some of the things He does." No part of my logical mind could formulate a good reason for turning the interview down. But trust is not about understanding God; it's about knowing God. Knowing that He sees the full picture of our lives, and has a well-calculated plan.

I applied for that job out of desperation, not faith. And I believe God allowed the interview opportunity to manifest as a test.

I was not filled with regret or fear, but instead I was filled with peace and excitement. I made peace with the decision to follow God and not my flesh and excitement about what better opportunity God has in store for me to further advance His purpose in my life.

Are you ready to say 'yes' to God? Take the prayer below, tweak it as needed and begin to pray and meditate on it. God will start to transform your heart.

God, I'm hearing a lot about surrendering and it scares me. I know you are a perfect God but what if you ask something of me, I cannot do or am unwilling to do? I know, I should give you total control over my life but I'm not sure I am ready. Give me the courage to do what I feel you calling me to do. Help me to know and understand that perfection is not what you seek but obedience. Give me a 'yes' heart, devoted to being at the center of your will. Remove my focus from fear to You. Thank you Lord, in the name of Jesus, Amen.

Focus & Reflect

....
....
....
....
....
....
....
....
....
....
....
....
....
....
....
....

DAY 19

Understanding the Character of God

"For as he thinks within himself, so is he."
–Proverbs 23:7

Background: Mostly written by Solomon, the purpose of Proverbs was to teach the people of Israel wisdom, how to attain it and apply it to everyday life. This chapter speaks on life and conduct.

"The mind is a powerful thing to waste." We've heard this statement a thousand time over. Yet, we over consume content that ultimately does more harm than good and under consume content that would stimulate our minds.

It's because of scriptures like this one in Proverbs and the Law of Attraction, people create vision boards and follow certain social media accounts, which visually represent things we desire, goals we want to achieve and places we want to go. But, what happens when those images stop being inspirational and become the thing that keeps us from obeying God? After all, He is the only one who can fulfill those very desires, beyond what we can even fathom.

There's a fine line between content serving as inspiration and motivation and it becoming a hindrance to our obedience to God.

We subconsciously become so driven by the images we consume, that when God tells us to do something that appears to lead us away from what we so desire, it seems way too hard. We already know what we want and how we want to achieve it. So, when God instructs us another way, it creates friction.

To make obeying God easier, we should do 3 things:

Truly understand the character of God

Stop caring about society's perception or the opinions of those around us

Not allow our personal expectations to be overly influenced by social 'norms'

Think about your closet friend for a moment. You know them well and trust their character. You value their opinions and input. What if you were that confident in the character of God? If we truly understood and believed the character of God, we'd see that obeying God is not as difficult.

Let's take a look at some of God's characteristics:

A Creator: (Elohim) Psalm 8:3; 19:1-6; 139:13-14, Genesis 1:1

All-Knowing: Romans 11:33-34, I Corinthians 2:16, Matthew 10:30

Friend (Philos): John 15:13

A Provider (Yahweh Yireh): Psalm 65:9-13; 145:16, Isaiah 25:4, Philippians 4:19

Peace (Yahweh Shalom) Judges 6:24, Colossians 3:15, I Peter 5:7, Philippians 4:7

The God Who Sees Us (El Roi): Genesis 16:13-14, Psalm 33:13-15, Proverbs 15:3

We can find comfort knowing that God is the same God today as He was then (Hebrews 13:8). The more we come to know, study and train our minds, the more we start to believe God for who He truly is and the easier it will become to obey Him.

Let me be clear: I struggle with obedience like everyone else. Ridding our minds of subconscious beliefs and destroying seeds of discontent, planted by the content we consume is challenging.

Complete the following sentence and pray over it/talk it out with God, and meditate on it throughout your week. Allow him to shatter those fears and bring you peace.

If I really believed God to be (insert a character(s) of His), then I would (insert what He has been calling you to do but you have been hesitant). My fear is that (insert what is hindering you).

Focus & Reflect

....

....

....

....

....

....

....

....

....

....

....

....

....

....

DAY 20

Exposed

*"When you ask, you do not receive, because you
ask with wrong motives, that you may spend what
you get on your pleasures." –James 4:3*

Background: The book of James was written to teach the correct Christian
behavior. In Chapter 4, we are encouraged to turn from our evil desires
and obey God. James also warns against trusting in our own plans and
possessions, over God.

The other day, I grabbed a bag of white cheddar popcorn from the pantry
in preparation for a night of movies and relaxation. Not to my surprise,
my dog started following me around. I looked back at her and said, "You're
following me around and this isn't even for you."

Then, God impressed upon my spirit this question: how many times have
we seen something or someone we wanted and chased after it even though
it wasn't meant for us?

There are times when the thing or person we want is simply outside of
God's will because it is bad for us, even though we might not yet see how.
However, God knows the beginning and the end and He is able to keep us
from heartache, failure and loss, if we listen to Him.

Other times, it's not that what we want is bad; it's why we want it. If our
motives are not pure, God will seek to expose to us what's in our heart
before blessing us with what we are seeking or working toward. We often

get so caught up in our desires that we fail to realize why we even want it. Sure, you want the promotion because you'll be making more money but what are the underlining reasons? Is it really because you want to prove someone wrong, or that you're better than someone else?

It's important that we do a heart check on why we desire what we do. Every level that God elevates us to, and every blessing that he gives, should be used to further His purpose in our lives and shed light on His name. It's not about us.

Take time in your conversation with God today and ask Him to reveal the motives behind the things you desire and to show you if any of your desires are not in alignment with His will for you. Lastly, ask for a surrendered heart and humble attitude to receive what He says.

Focus & Reflect

....

....

....

....

....

....

....

....

....

....

....

....

....

....

....

DAY 21

Authentic Love

"We know what real love is because Jesus gave up His life for us..." –1 John 3:16

Background: The purpose of 1 John, written by the apostle John, was to reassure Christians in their faith and to counter false teachings. In Chapter 3, John points out that we are the children of God, and because of this, we live a certain way. One of the fruits of being God's child is showing love, just as He showed His love for us.

[Alexa, play "Real Love" by Mary J. Blige] How many of us have searched for are searching for a real love in a person? Ironically, we've had real love since before our lives ever began on earth (Job 10:10-12). Jesus has loved us since Day 1. We can be sure of His love, because He shows us daily and He gave up His life for us. Not only did He give up a lavish life in heaven by coming to earth, but He gave up his physical life by enduring a dreadful death on the cross. Jesus freely gave up his life for us, the greatest act of love (John 15:13).

Sometimes when life deals us a bad hand, we can find ourselves looking to God asking why. If He loves us, then why does he allow certain things to happen? We might get an answer, or we might not. However, we can't be tricked into thinking He does not love us. There's no way He would sacrifice His life for each of us, without truly loving us. Imagine laying your life down for someone you don't truly love. You wouldn't.

No matter how difficult life gets at times, we can't allow Satan to place doubts in our mind about God's love for us. Instead, we should ask God to remind us of His love and to help us feel the magnitude of His love, despite how life might look right now. He has a perfect plan for each of us. Rest assured that everything He allows to happen in life, He will use in a great way (Romans 8:28).

Having a relationship with God is amazing! However, like with any relationship, there will be trials. But the trials we face in our relationship with God will always serve a purpose, and are never indicators that He doesn't love us. When we allow for it, trials will grow us and strengthen our bond with Him (James 1:2-4). Remember, He is walking with us every step of the way.

If you are currently going through something or feeling unloved by God, spend some transparent time in prayer, expressing your doubts. Let Him in and tell Him why you doubt His love. Take an honest look at your circumstances. Could you be where we are as a result of disobedience? If so, repent and ask for forgiveness. End by asking Him to send you a postcard reminding you of His love for you. Now, wait with expectancy for Him to reveal His love to you in a fresh way!

Focus & Reflect

DAY 22

Put Your Best Foot Forward

"If anyone competes as an athlete, he does not win the prize unless he competes according to the rules." – II Timothy 2:5

*"Run in such a way that you may win."
– I Corinthians 9:24*

Background: 1 Corinthians, written by Paul, was meant to teach believers how to live for Christ. In the chapter, he highlights the skills needed to live a successful Christian life. II Timothy was also written by Paul but to encourage Timothy. In II Timothy, Paul wanted Timothy to know that despite facing sufferings, he was capable of enduring. He uses the analogy of an athlete to make his point.

Thinking back to my days as a track athlete, it's amazing how much hard work I put into becoming a great one. In high school I trained all year around, sometimes twice a day. Despite how hard it was I knew it would pay off and I would be a better athlete. I also understood that the harder I worked, the greater the chances were that I would get a collegiate scholarship.

There were many days throughout those times that I didn't feel like practicing or giving my all but I didn't want to let my coaches or my parents down. I spent hours with my coaches every day and respected them and the time they chose to spend with me. I was confident in their abilities and respected their authority.

Do we understand God's authority? Do we respect it? How important is it for us to please Him? Do we really believe He knows and is capable as the leader of our lives? Imagine if we spent more time with God. We would adopt the same attitude of not wanting to let Him down and we would trust Him more.

If we're honest, we treat a lot of God's commands as if they're options. Yes, we have free will but we should obey God at all times. I had free will at track practice, but I still completed my workouts as I was told. Today, you have free will at your job but you still do what is required of you.

We are each running our own unique race. If we expect to win, we have to put in the work. We have to show up to practice every day and give it our all. Let's go HARD for God! No matter how hard the race is, don't quit and don't slack up.

Think about where God has you right now. Are you running to win? How can you go harder with the task/race God has you in?

Focus & Reflect

No More Excuses

*"But Moses pleaded with the Lord, 'O Lord, I'm
not very good with words. I never have been, and
I'm not now, even though you have spoken to me.
I get tongue-tied, and my words get tangled.' Then
the Lord asked Moses, "Who makes a person's
mouth? Who decides whether people speak or do
not speak, hear or do not hear, see or do not see?
Is it not I, the Lord? Now go! I will be with you as
you speak, and I will instruct you in what to say."*
–Exodus 4:10-12

Background: In the previous chapter, God told Moses that he would be the
one to lead the Israelites out of Egypt. His first order of business was to go
before Pharaoh and demand that He let the people go. In the verse above,
we read one of the few objections Moses has.

A lot of times when God gives us a vision or a dream, it can be scary. In the
beginning stages of my business I doubted my ability to succeed. I saw all
my inadequacies and how disqualified I was. What I failed to realize at the
time is that God-sized dreams require God's strength and access.

When God assigns us to something, our inadequacies are irrelevant. He
knows our strengths and weaknesses and will bridge the gap where we cannot. Our job is to keep our focus and our dependency on Him, at all times.

We should not worry about the 'how.' Our only concern and effort should go toward what He has told us to do.

God will put us in positions that will require us to use skills we might not have or that need to be developed. The only way you develop or strengthen your muscles is by working them out, just as you gain endurance by running. He will continue to place us in positions that stretch us until that weakness is strengthened. If God placed dreams in us that were small, we would not need Him. His desire is to be in close relationship with us, so He will put us in positions that will bring us closer to Him

Don't be afraid to dream God-sized dreams. Don't push out ideas that come to mind because you think they're too big or you're not good enough to make it happen

It's not our abilities or credentials that qualifies us. God, the One who sends us, is who qualifies us. He will open doors to opportunities we thought we would never see and surround us with people to help us that we never thought we'd even be in the same room in. Don't limit God.

Take time to think over your life and write out at least three times when God surprised you and made a way out of no way. Know that He is still that same God today and is ready to take you to new heights that you've never imagined.

Focus & Reflect

....

....

....

....

....

....

....

....

....

....

....

....

....

....

....

....

....

DAY 24
False Expectations

"Are you the Messiah we've been expecting or
should we keep looking for someone else?"
–Matthew 11:3

Background: John the Baptist had been preparing the way for Jesus' arrival and was preaching that when He came, He would come in a mighty way, judging the sins of the world. However, when He came, He was gentle and preached a message of love, not judgment. In this verse, John the Baptist is speaking to Jesus and questioning if He is in fact the Messiah.

Placing expectations on God can be dangerous. When God called me into a season of singleness, He made it clear that it was for me to grow and mature, mentally and spiritually. When He called me out of singleness, immediately I started thinking it meant the next person I would meet would be my husband. I mean God wouldn't call me off the dating bench after 4 years for any other reason, right? After all, I had made it clear to God many of times that the next person I dated, I wanted to be my husband. I did not have time to waste dating around. Nope, not me!

Do you notice something? It was all about what "I" wanted, what "I" expected, what "I" had planned. My expectation was once I opened myself up to dating, boom, I'd find my husband to-be! So imagine when things didn't go that way. I was looking up to God like, "what's up?" I was confused, disappointed and angry. I acted as if God had let me down, as if He had not honored His word. But when I looked back on how I got to that point, I realized something. God never told me that was His plan. He simply called me off the bench; He didn't give me the play. (Or, I didn't stick around long enough to hear it) So, the only person I should have been upset with was myself.

We have to be careful about placing expectations on our obedience. Growing up, when our parents told us to do something, we did it without expectation. The same should be true in our obedience to God. We should not expect to get rewarded for doing what He tells us to do. And we definitely shouldn't paint a picture of what we think the result of our obedience will be. We can't attach terms to our obedience.

We should live life fully surrendered to Him. Whatever he asks of us, we should do so willingly, without expectations. Yes, He is intentional and always has a plan but wait until He reveals to you what that plan is.

Have you subconsciously put expectations on your obedience to Him? Ask God to help you rid yourself of your expectations and to reveal to you what His plans and desires are for you. Consider confiding in a friend that will hold you accountable to not place terms on your obedience to God.

....

....

....

....

....

....

....

....

....

....

....

....

....

....

....

DAY 25

We All Need Someone

*"Therefore encourage one another and build up
one another, just as you also are doing."*
–I Thessalonians 5:11

Background: Paul wrote this letter to the church at Thessalonica to strengthen them in their faith and encourage them as they waited for Christ's return. One thing he stresses is to always be prepared for the return of Christ. In this verse, He encourages them to continue helping each other live accordingly.

In our earthly relationships, there are times when we don't feel like spending time with a person, being selfless or putting in much effort. But if we expect to maintain a healthy relationship, we have to fight through it, so that it does not become the narrative.

Likewise, we will have to fight for our relationship with God. There will be days when we don't feel like picking up our Bible, we don't feel like praying, going to church or listening to any spiritual music. We just don't feel it. But if we don't fight during those days, then those days turn into seasons. Trust me, I know all too well.

Not long ago, I was having one of those days. My mood was low and I didn't feel like doing anything. I talked to my best friend and she encouraged me by telling me to go workout, listen to a recorded episode from one of my favorite podcasts and a sermon she had sent me. I didn't want to hear the advice and was even less enthused about taking her up on it. But I did because I knew she would follow up with me. It is imperative to surround yourself with like-minded people who will push you and keep it real with you. Make sure to lean on those people, don't take them for granted and simply have them in your life as fixtures.

I fought that day. I fought through my low vibe, and sad energy and God met me half way. He picked me up and carried me through the rest of the day. Just like we expect our partners or friends to meet us half way in relationships, God wants us to put in the effort and meet him halfway. Bad days will come, but you've got to fight through them, don't run from them, and don't let them overtake you. Fight!

Identify one or two people in your life that you know you can trust to help you in your relationship with Christ. Take those names to God and begin to ask Him what areas in your life they will best hold you accountable in. Also, ask that He help you be transparent and receptive of their accountability and that they would be diligent and fearless in holding you accountable.

Focus & Reflect

DAY 26

Are You Listening?

"Call to Me, and I will answer you, and show you great and mighty things, which you do not know."
–Jeremiah 33:3

Background: These are the words that God spoke to Jeremiah while he was in prison. In this chapter, God is giving Jeremiah reassurance that the Jews would be restored, despite their current circumstances. In the same way God promised to answer Jeremiah, He will answer our calls to Him.

Have you ever been with a friend, ready to tell them something exciting? But they are immersed in their phone, texting and scrolling through social media. Now your excitement is replaced with irritation and slight disappointment. Despite what they say, you know they are not fully engaged and will miss certain parts of your story. They'll ask to repeat certain things or even worse later in the day ask you, "now what were you saying about…"

We always want to hear from God, whether it's the plans He has for us, direction we are seeking or the green light to move forward with something. And He wants to tell us these things! But imagine His disappointment when we are not positioned to hear from Him. We are asking but never stop to listen. We are constantly doing things throughout the day, never pausing long enough to listen or spend time in His presence, being still. We somehow expect to hear from God in between working, caring for our family, texting, surfing social media, working out, watching TV, listening to music and socializing.

Before God speaks to us, He needs to know we are listening. And before we can hear His voice and receive His instruction, our hearts need to be surrendered to Him. When God speaks to us and we have not yet surrendered to Him, we run the risk of not fully committing to His instruction.

God is always communicating with us. When He is not, He is waiting for us to position ourselves to hear Him and our hearts to receive His word.

If you are waiting to hear from God on something specific, ask yourself two things:

Have I put myself in a position to hear from Him?

If His answer is not what I want it to be, am I ready to obey anyways?

Start dedicating some quiet time each day to spend in His presence. Quiet the noise so you can hear from Him. Begin asking God to help you surrender your plans to Him and prepare your heart for His perfect will. As you wait to hear from Him, seek out what it is He wants you to be doing now, right where you are.

Focus & Reflect

....

....

....

....

....

....

....

....

....

....

....

....

....

....

....

DAY 27

All Bark, No Bite

"All right, you may test him," the Lord said to
Satan. "Do whatever you want with everything he
possesses, but don't harm him physically." So Satan
left the Lord's presence." –Job 1:12

Background: In this passage, Satan approaches God, looking for who he may attack. He did not and still does not have the authority to act without God. Here, God grants Satan permission to attack Job but with boundaries. God knew that Job would overcome this and that his testimony would bring Him glory.

I was walking Star, my 54lb Pit Bull, and we passed another dog that couldn't have been more than 10lbs. The dog was leashed but still attempted to make its way toward us, barking incessantly. Star paused briefly, glanced over its way and then continued on, unbothered.

From that brief interaction, I was reminded of two things. One, just like that dog was on a leash and couldn't get to my dog, God has Satan on a leash. He cannot attack us unless God gives him permission. (I encourage you to study the story of Job for more on this topic.) He will attempt to scare us or incite fear in us but has no actual power over us, or our situation. We give him power when we give in to his scare tactics and lies. When we allow Satan's "bark" to deter us from what God is calling us to do, we sabotage ourselves and sometimes, miss out on or delay the opportunities and blessings God has for us. The truth is, if my dog were to approach the smaller dog, it would retreat back to its owner. Think about what would happen if we spoke God's promises against Satan's attack, he would have no choice but to retreat!

The second thing I learned from Star that day is how I should respond to Satan when he barks. After quickly assessing there was no real danger, she continued on with her walk, unbothered by the threats of the other dog. When doubts, fear and negative self-talk show up on your walk with God, assess it for what it is: tactics deployed by the devil to keep you from obeying God and fulfilling your purpose. Once you assess it for what it is, you can keep moving forward, unbothered.

Small dogs bark out of fear when they see larger dogs. Satan barks out of fear when he sees you walking in or toward the will of God for your life. Don't fall victim to the threats of a being that is smaller and less powerful than you. You are a child of God, He dwells in you and His power has been activated in you. There is no reason to fear or be tricked into thinking that you cannot accomplish the assignment He has given you.

Type out 2 or 3 affirmations and/or scriptures to keep handy in your phone. Use them as reminders to yourself and the devil who watches over you and the power that is within you. You can even take it one step further and print them out and display them in your living space as a daily reminder.

Focus & Reflect

DAY 28

Respect the Process

"So he sent and brought him in. Now, he was ruddy, with beautiful eyes and a handsome appearance. And the Lord said, 'Arise, anoint him; for this is he.'" -I Samuel 16:12

Background: After the death of Saul, God sends Samuel to Bethlehem to visit Jesse and his sons. Among Jesse's sons, God has selected one of them to be King of Israel. We read in verse 12, that it is Jesse's youngest son, who God has chosen.

When God gives us a promise or gives us a vision of where He is taking us, we often neglect to think about the road to getting there. When God laid the vision in my heart of having my own business, I knew starting a business would be difficult but I did not really think about the journey to the position of simply getting started. There were many battles I had to fight just to get to the starting point. There is a process to everything. If we get too far ahead of God in our heads, we can easily be discouraged when we face battles or trials, as we move toward where God has called us.

David knew at a young age he would be King (I Samuel 16:13). I'm sure he knew it would be a challenging job. However, I wonder if he thought much about how the road to becoming King would be? We now know that before he was appointed King, he would first serve in the King's court, fight Goliath, be the commander of King Saul's army and hide from King Saul after receiving death threats from him. Even at that point, he was only the King of Judah. It would be another seven years before Israel and Judah would become one and he would rule over all.

Now, don't get discouraged and think you'll be waiting some 30-40 years before you receive what God has for you. Everyone's journey is different. However, the bigger the promise is the more preparation required. Because we don't see all the moving pieces involved with our lives and everything God does to make things happen, we forget the intricacies involved with painting the backdrop of our lives. What I love about David's story are the amazing wins God allowed him to have along the way to becoming king. Sometimes we can get so focused on where we are headed, that we neglect to see and appreciate the victories along the way.

Along David's journey, he went from being a lowly shepherd boy, underestimated by his father, to living in the King's court as a musician, to becoming a celebrated warrior (I Samuel 17), respected as a righteous man of God, to becoming King. What an amazing journey! There were unfavorable times during the journey as well but they did not compare to the victories.

Take time to list out the victories (small or big) and fun experiences you've had along your journey thus far. It's far too easy to look at life and recount the challenging times, so really put the effort and time into your list. As you start listing out things, you will start to see the hand of God woven throughout your journey.

Focus & Reflect

DAY 29

When Blessings Become Burdens

"...always giving thanks to God the Father for everything, in the name of our Lord Jesus Christ."
–Ephesians 5:20

Background: Paul wrote this letter to the church at Ephesus to encourage the Christians in their relationship with God. In the first part of chapter 5 (v.1-21), he outlines how we should live our lives as the children of God.

So, you've finally been blessed with that thing you've been praying for, but what has your reaction been so far?

You would think that after praying long and hard for something, we'd be in a posture of praise when God comes through. However, a lot of times, we just complain. We pray for a promotion only to later complain about the time commitment. We pray for marriage only to complain about the planning and expenses of the wedding. We pray for new clients and then complain when we have to adjust our schedules to accommodate them. The list goes on. I've personally been guilty of this myself.

Let's not turn our blessings into burdens. Sometimes I imagine God looks down at us and thinks, 'So, did you want that blessing or not?' Other times, I think He looks down at us and His heart is saddened that after

He's removed obstacles and given us a favor, we use the same mouths we petitioned with, to complain with.

Take at least 5 minutes or the drive on your way to work to reflect on the blessings you've turned into burdens. Ask God to forgive you for your ungratefulness and to give you a fresh outlook on what He has done for you. Ask him to change the posture of your heart from complaint to praise.

Focus & Reflect

....

....

....

....

....

....

....

....

....

....

....

....

....

....

....

....

DAY 30

God's Consistent Love

"Greater love has no man than this, than to lay down one's life for his friends." –John 15:13

Background: Jesus speaks to his disciples, as He prepares them for his death.

God's love is truly like no other. His love has seen me through depression, not wanting to live, reckless living and even anger directed toward Him. I have both, inadvertently and intentionally, shut God out. I've hurt Him more times than I can remember and taken advantage of His grace and unconditional love.

Not long before starting this devotional, I found myself in a season of being angry with God. I wasn't praying, reading my bible or going to church. And unlike other times of not being motivated, this time I didn't care. It was almost intentional. I wasn't asking my friends to pray for me about it and when they offered, internally I wish they hadn't. I was good. I was going to live life on my own terms. A few months passed and I begin to really feel God tug on my heart to let Him back in. Slowly but surely, I came around. Through my sobbing tears I found myself asking God to forgive me for turning my back on Him and admitting to Him that I desperately needed Him. I couldn't "do life" on my own like I had somehow convinced myself I could. You'll never guess what God's response was.

It's like He picked me up off the floor, gathered me in His arms and show-ered me with His love and peace. He didn't make reconnecting with Him difficult. He did not hide from me. He loved me harder, grabbed my hand

and led me out of the trenches. He healed me. He showed me His love like never before. Months later, I went on a 40 day fast and He allowed me to experience Him still, in even greater ways. It was during that time that this devotional thought was birthed. God could have turned His back on me; He could've chosen not to speak His words, these words on these very pages, to me. I turned my back on God but He never turned His on me. I've never known a love like that. Anyone else would have walked away from me, and rightfully so. But God's love is unconditional, pure, refreshing and compelling.

I don't know what your story is but God does and He loves you in spite of it all. He's here for you, in your presence, even now as you read these words. Maybe you're in a situation you feel you don't deserve to be in and maybe you're angry with God or questioning His love for you. Hundreds of people can tell you He loves you, you can hear numerous sermons on His love, you can even read the words in this devotional that say He loves you. But it's not until you let Him in, that you will experience it for yourself and come to know His one of a kind love. As people, we all have boundaries on our love. But God's love knows no boundaries. Turn to Him; let Him shower you with His love. He is waiting.

If you are questioning God's love or are yearning to experience His love in fresh ways, you have to invite Him in. You have to give Him the opportunity to show you His love. Pray with this prayer:

"God, your love is written about throughout the bible and I know that as the greatest sign of your love, you gave your son for me. Sometimes though, I still don't feel loved by You. Life does not look like how I thought it would or how I think it should. I've done things I'm not pleased about and have even shut you out at times. And honestly God, there have been times that I have felt let down by You. I want to know your love; I want to experience your love in a new and fresh way. Work on my heart God, so that I am in a position to receive your love. Reveal the things in my life that are stopping me from experiencing You. Thank you Lord, in the name of Jesus I pray, amen."

Focus & Reflect

....
....
....
....
....
....
....
....
....
....
....
....
....
....
....
....
....
....